Shared Memories

Reminiscences by the

50-Plus Springfield Inter-Community Group

compiled by
Michael Hall

Published March 2003 by Island Publications
132 Serpentine Road, Newtownabbey, Co Antrim BT36 7JQ
© Michael Hall 2003

ISBN 1 899510 41 9

Farset Community Think Tanks Project is funded by:
The EU Special Support Programme for Peace and Reconciliation
administered through the **Northern Ireland Community Relations Council**

The 50-Plus Springfield Inter-Community Group
was formed through the merger of
Highfield Women's 50-Plus Group and
Springfield Senior Citizens Group

Their reminiscence sessions took place at
Highfield Community Centre
facilitated by Ann Vallely and Robert Sterrit

Printed by Regency Press, Belfast

Introduction

Aside from the many personal tragedies which occurred during the course of Northern Ireland's three decades of 'Troubles', one of the saddest consequences of the violence was the break-up of relatively mixed neighbourhoods, when people of one religion or the other were either forced, or felt it necessary, to move to 'safer' areas. Although some courageous individuals endeavoured to maintain long-established relationships, the ongoing violence and its increasing intensity gradually imposed rigid demarcation lines between communities, which few dared cross without a great deal of anxiety.

Throughout those dark days, numerous community groups arose within each area which endeavoured to provide badly needed support networks. And, in recent years, especially since the advent of the 'peace process', many such community groups, originating from both sides of the communal divide, have been brought increasingly into contact with one another.

This is what happened with the members of Highfield Women's 50-Plus Group. In the course of different cross-community social events they frequently encountered the women of Springfield Senior Citizens Group. The members of the two groups found they had much in common. They had all grown up within the same area of West Belfast, even if it now possessed a 'sectarian interface'. They had all been in their late teens or early twenties at the beginning of the Troubles. They had socialised and shopped in each other's areas when such interaction was commonplace – religious differences had not stopped Protestants from attending céilis, or Catholics from shopping on the Shankill Road. Furthermore, some remembered as children a time when Protestants and Catholics huddled together into air-raid shelters to avoid Hitler's bombers.

Because of this bond, the two groups decided to merge into one: the 50-Plus Springfield Inter-Community Group. In late 2002, facilitated by Highfield Community Centre, they requested that Farset Community Think Tanks Project record a series of 'reminiscence evenings', in the hope that a pamphlet depicting some of their shared memories would have an important message for the wider society.

Michael Hall *Farset Community Think Tanks Project*

Undivided Memories

Growing up

All the members of the group had vivid recollections of their early days, although memories of school were not always positive.

> There wasn't many from our areas went to grammar school. You could get what they called a scholarship, but you were very lucky if you got it.
>
> Girls were never encouraged to think about educating themselves. People said: "They're wasting their money educating you."
>
> When I was fourteen I left school on a Friday and was working in Blackstaff [Mill] on Monday. Straight out of school and into work.
>
> I was too.
>
> Your ma was waiting on your wages in them days.
>
> I never learned nothing at school but yet I loved school.
>
> Oh, I hated school.
>
> No, I loved school.
>
> All I done was run messages for the nuns, 'cause I lived beside the convent. And I was running all up and down Clonard Street, going for their black market stuff and going for this or that, or the 'pennies for the black babies'. I'd to carry it up every Friday and get the key to lock it away... I thought that was great, going messages. But that was my education. Our ones will say to me now: "Ma, did you learn nothing?" And here's me: "No."
>
> That's another thing: you had to give money for the 'black babies' and yet your mother and father really hadn't any money to give away.
>
> My mother used to say: "There's plenty of wee babies at home."
>
> In St. John's school, we used to have to bring money over for the coal for the fire, do you remember that?
>
> And you weren't allowed to go to the toilet without permission.
>
> Yes, you had to put your hand up and sit until they decided to let you go, and ours was out in the yard too – it was freezing.

Memories from teenage and adolescent years seemed much more positive.

> My friend and I used to go into the city centre. And the Salvation Army would be out every Sunday night. They'd this big screen up with all the hymns written up: 'Give me five minutes more' or 'You are my sunshine'... and we'd stand and sing away to them. But this night the captain suddenly announces: "We have two young ladies here who I've noticed have been coming for a lot of months now, and we'd like them to tell their stories." Then he walked over towards us! The two of us flew off like the hammers, and never went back again!
>
> The Salvation Army always had good music.
>
> Aye, I used to go down and sing away.
>
> It was somewhere to go on a Sunday night.
>
> I went to Sunday school on Sunday, and then to church that night.

For one participant, religious affiliation certainly presented no barrier to the pursuit of enjoyment.

> You had to be dressed up to go to our church, with your hat and all on. The service ended at eight o'clock but as soon as I came out the hat came off and I was away up to Ardoyne to the céili! If I didn't go the céili I went to the jig in Coates Street. And if I didn't come in before half-ten I was near getting murdered and told: "You'll not be getting out next week!"
>
> St. Paul's Parish always had a pantomime, and when I was about fourteen they let us all take part in it even though we couldn't sing or dance or nothing. It was lovely – Aladdin, and things like that – and you thought it was great being a chorus girl. They couldn't pay you because it was just the church, so in return they let you in to church activities for free for a year, which meant I was at St. Paul's every night; you went and done everything with all the other girls – I thought it was great.
>
> Remember Jimmy Craigen – he acted the dame, and he'd wear two electric light bulbs on his ears? We thought the costumes were fantastic.
>
> But the stage in the hall was that high, if you'd fallen off when you were dancing I think you would have been killed; it seemed like ten feet to us.
>
> I often wondered how older people knew all the words of so many songs. They'd no TV then, and very few had a radio.
>
> They used to have song sheets.
>
> And they used to be in the paper, the *Empire* used to give all the different songs out every Sunday.
>
> A family in our street was one of the first to get a TV, and us youngsters would go there; they allowed us all in.

We usually went to the cinema: the Clonard, the Diamond, and the Arcadian.

I went to the Stadium every Saturday for fourpence.

The Stadium was lovely, but you had to queue for ages round the outside to get into it.

The Stadium was luxury compared to the Clonard or the Diamond, you'd have needed waterboots for the Diamond! You see if anybody ever needed to go to the toilet they just did it where they were! The woman who owned it – Kate McCann, you called her – would go up and down each row of seats with a big torch trying to catch anybody who had done it. I was sitting there this evening and the next thing I felt was something wet, and I let out a yell and, of course, Kate was down immediately with the torch. But by the time she got there the whole row behind us was empty!

Where you ever in the Central?

I was, that was another place where you'd have needed a paddle.

What! You'd have needed a *boat* for the Central!

The Windsor was nice too, and the Broadway was swanky.

I didn't like the Savoy, but I always loved the Crumlin.

I never really liked the pictures much; I preferred going to dances.

No, I loved the aul' pictures.

But see when you were courting, where else could you go? You danced maybe at the weekend, but during the week if you'd a date you went to the pictures, to the Imperial or the Regent.

You stood in the queue and you were entertained by all the singers.

Then as now, finding a 'fella' and courting were important activities for young women.

Many people went up the 'mountain loaney' for a fresh drink from the stream, but I didn't, I went up there to do my courting.

So did I. You hadn't always money for pictures or pubs in them days, even for dances, so we went up there. Anyway, sure there was no need for fancy places for courting.

I remember when I was about eighteen, and we used to go out dancing on Friday and Saturday nights, we used to go down to the Spanish Rooms on the Falls...

Where they sold the 'scrumpy'?

Aye. Anyway, this day, before we went to the dance, me and my mates were walking down and I happened to turn round – but who's getting off the bus only my mother and father! Here's me: "Oh, don't let on we were heading for the Spanish Rooms, let on we're walking on up the street." But when I looked round them two were going into the Spanish Rooms as well! They went downstairs and we went upstairs.

I always went to Coates Street for the dances. They were good dancers in there.

I remember I used to sneak out of work on a Wednesday afternoon to go to the Plaza.

The Coconut Grove, wasn't that another one?

Or the Orchid, it came on to be nice now, but before that it was called the Rotunda.

There was plenty of places to go, wasn't there?

What did you call the one on Donegal Street?

Clarks?

No, no. It had an aul' wooden floor...

Paradise.

I never went round there. I went to the céilis from when I was fourteen to when I was sixteen.

I think everybody went to those.

Wouldn't you love to be young again? Would you not like to be young again? And to know what you know now?

You'd probably want all the fancy things that the kids today want.

I don't think so, somehow.

Courting was not without its problem, however...

My father would have stood at the door and said to the fella: "Have you no home to go to? It's time she was in." And he would have stood there until I came in, like.

My chum had to be in for ten o'clock, and we used to have to run down York Street to get home in time. And one day I said to myself: 'What am *I* running for? I don't have to be in until half-ten!'

I used to take my sister to the dances with me and she met this fella of a different religion, so she wasn't allowed to go home with him. And I said to her: "Look, when you're coming home, meet me at the post box just up the street, don't go into the house without me." Of course, I comes back one night and there was no sign of her and I thought she was already home, so I went on into the house, only to find she hadn't arrived back at all. I thought: 'how am I going to get her into the house?', for my mother and father slept downstairs. Now, my other sister was very house-proud, wouldn't have an empty milk bottle sitting in the house, and I wakened her and said: "When Florence gets back you go down and let on you're putting milk bottles out and open the door for her to creep in." I had to wait at the window for Florence to arrive, then whisper: "Stand there till Jean opens the door." On another occasion I told her to go up the entry and I would sneak her in the back door. And we were doing everything quietly until she fell over a mop bucket and wakened the whole house!

Fashion, health and pawnshops

Dressing up for such activities was an important part of the experience.

I remember one time deciding to try dressmaking. Our Ursula bought this lovely satiny material, with a Chinese-type pattern. I says I'll make two dresses for the night – with a split down the side. I nearly had to push our Thora into hers, she couldn't breathe in it, but I made her wear it. Here's me: "You're going out in it, I spent all night making it!" I thought they were lovely.

Do you remember 'bell skirts'? You couldn't get enough petticoats to make them sit out... and big stiletto heels.

People got a lot of things made from dressmakers then, so you did.

We used to go to Mary Buckle; she used to make all the things, she was in Percy Street.

Remember Mrs Mason done the kashmir knitting? Or Rita Mason.

There used to be a great dressmaker over at Bridge End.

You see, you didn't buy off the peg then.

Lally McKinny in Leoville Street made coats. They were tailoresses, they made coats, like; you had to be a tailoress to make a coat.

But most people bought material and made it themselves.

Anybody that went to the stitching at fourteen was always very handy with the machine, learned to sew.

I always envied those girls who were able to use a sewing machine.

I never fussed too much, I wore the same thing, every week when I went out; people had to make do with a lot less then.

'Making-do' impacted on different aspects of everyday life.

We used to use flour bags as pillow cases, but we could never get the designs washed out of them.

I think they were sixpence each, those flour bags.

And your da's big overcoat was thrown on top of your bed at night.

Sure that's what Billy Connolly said, that there was sleeves in his duvet!

You needed everything on top of you, 'cause I remember it being freezing, there was no central heating then.

Your coal fire had to heat the whole house.

Your mummy baked soda bread. And she baked on Hallowe'en, a big pudding...

They're all bought now from the shop.

It wasn't all cheerful – there was a lot of tuberculosis in those days...

Aye, there was. There was one family near us, and I don't how many coffins came out of their house – about seven – all the brothers and sisters, one after the other. Consumption, they called it then.

Galloping consumption.

Nevertheless, despite problems like TB and work-related illnesses, the group members felt that people then actually led healthier lifestyles.

People walked everywhere in those days.

On a Sunday afternoon, we always used to go for a long walk, especially in the good weather. I remember walking to Greencastle.

I remember on a Sunday night walking up the Glen Road and right down to Andersonstown, and back home again. And sometimes my mate and I would get two boys, like, and if we liked them we went to the picture house or something with them on the Monday night.

The food and all was a lot healthier then as well. You got porridge for your breakfast, and that was good for you. Hardly any kids would eat porridge for you nowadays.

And the vegetables and potatoes wouldn't have been sprayed with all that stuff that's on them now. And you'd no fridge, so everything was eat that day and your mummy went out the next morning to do more shopping.

Aye, if she'd the money.

There was nothing left the next morning; nothing was wasted, it was all eaten.

People never asked for much, sure they didn't? But then again, they didn't get much either.

You always had a good set of clothes for wearing to Mass on Sunday.

All the same, you didn't really have to dress up that much for Mass, you would have saw people going to Mass in their slippers.

Sure, but you'd a better set of clothes on Sunday than you had for the rest of the week.

Mention of a 'best set of clothes' led inevitably to discussion of that once ubiquitous aspect of working-class life – the pawnshop.

You had a good set of clothes for Sunday, and mine always went into the pawn on Monday and out again on Saturday... you wore it on Sunday then it went back in again on Monday.

Everybody had to use the pawn in those days.

Oh God, aye, my mother used it all the time.

Everybody did, more or less.

My sister Bell and I had two coats exactly the same, and the woman who lived next door to us was stuck for her rent money this day, and my mother lent her what she thought was Bell's coat to take to the pawn, but it was actually mine... and there was three pound in the pocket!

My da once sent me to the pawn to pawn my child's clothes, 'cause he needed money for fags. But when I got there I thought: 'Why should I friggin' pawn my own child's clothes for him!' So when I got back and he says: "Have you got the money?" I told him: "I'm not pawning my child's clothes! You drunk the money, let your drinking mates get you the fags... 'cause I'm not!"

Despite the poverty I think there was more of a community spirit in those days.

Oh yes, your door was never locked.

You shared your stew and you shared your soup, and if your bone had a good bit of bristle on it, it went from pot to pot.

Sometimes when you think back on it all, you wonder how poor people survived in those days.

There was a cycle of bad debt nearly in every home, 'cause people were all caught up in the 'Co-quarter'.

Oh, the 'Co-quarters'! I remember them days!

And that's when the pawnshops done well, 'cause you had to pay the Co-op every thirteen weeks, so all your stuff was pawned to pay the Co and then after that you breathed again.

They called it 'Co-itis'!

Manys a woman topped themselves over it. There would always have been a suicide or two coming up to the 'Co-quarter'.

Some of those debts were handed down to the daughters as well.

And then there were the money lenders. Some of them held onto your family allowance book and they cashed it for you.

My mother maybe got her milk and coal from the 'Co', but that was all... but she would get nothing else, she was so scared of getting into debt.

Comradeship at the workplace

Work was remembered both for its worrying scarcity at times, and the opportunities for friendship it offered when available.

During the depression many men couldn't find regular work.

It was especially hard during the 'hungry thirties'.

My father was with the DOE; he worked on the roads, digging roads. They only got the 'outdoor relief' for the work they done, and there was no stopping when it rained.

Well, my daddy worked in McGladry's brick yard – McGladry was a millionaire – but they got thirty shillings and if it rained they got nothing. They didn't get 'rained off' money... and that was terrible for them poor men.

As for working in Mackies, that was white slavery.

Aye, my daddy worked in the fretting shop, in the foundry; he used to come home looking like a coalman and ended up with 'Mackies dust'.

But at least when my father had work, he always brought his money home and gave it to my mother, which was one good thing.

I worked in the mill.

I worked in the ropeworks

I worked in the Shankill for a quare while, I worked in a sweetie shop there. I got my wedding cake and all on the Shankill – from Trimbles.

I worked in a tabulating factory, in Castlereagh.

I worked in Jessella and then I worked in C&A. I worked in C&A for twenty years, all but three months, and loved every minute of it, it was great fun.

I was working from I was fourteen in an office over in Short Strand, that was my first job. I went to commercial school for shorthand and typing, and I went from that to Inglis's office in Elisa Street, and then from that to the Ever-Ready Company in Bankmore Street. I got married from there and I was married sixteen years when I took twelve hours a week in the C&A; that's where I met Martha. I was there for seventeen years.

Aye, we some great times there.

Didn't C&A go down very quick?

It did, unfortunately. But it was a great firm to work for.

Aye, I only worked twelve hours a week, and I contributed to nothing yet I came out with a lump sum and a wee pension. They were very, very good.

I went into the hospital to work and when I was there about three weeks the ward sister asked me where I had worked before. I told her I had worked in the mill. And I asked her if there was something wrong, but she said: "No, you're doing the job so well; we love to see youse ones come into the hospital, then we know the place will be kept clean."

I worked in the carding room... I could draw and rove and comb, but there was an awful aul dust.

Aye, it got in your hair and all.

And you'd have smelt it off you a mile away.

You'd see the wee boys out playing on Clonard Street, on their break, and they were a yellow colour, and they were in their bare feet 'cause it was water they were standing in. They were about fourteen years old.

That would have been the spinning room. There was wet spinning and dry spinning.

Shopping and perming

The current proliferation of massive out-of-town shopping centres has gone hand in hand with the demise of local shops and facilities.

In those days you went anywhere if you wanted to shop. We always walked over to the Shankill, 'cause we liked all the shops there.

My mummy went to Hollands the butcher at the top of Canmore Street.

And Sylvia's – that was a great shop.

And the 'real McCoy' – she said everything was the real McCoy.

Do you remember the first pawnshop just as you went over the hill in Sandy Row? They also did Beltex 'seconds' – you know, kids' stuff. They were awful dear to buy new, but he done seconds; it was brilliant, I pushed the pram over the hill to that pawn shop all the time.

Aye, Sandy Row was another good place for shopping, though there's not much left there now.

Highfield's the same, there's only the one shop there now and we had no chemist for a long time. And we're only just getting a local doctor.

Yet at one time we'd everything, a post office... everything.

But sure the owners couldn't keep the shops going, they were being robbed all the time. The corner shops have become extinct because of robberies.

Before the 'Troubles' there were forty shops on the Springfield, forty shops right along it. Yet we've only about three there now, though we're getting a new chip shop.

It used to be great; if you run out of something you could just go down the Springfield at any time of the day.

Do you remember Donnelly's shop up in Springfield? He sold all his stuff straight out of the boxes. He never got time to take the stuff out of the boxes and put them onto the shelves.

I remember him well; we used to do our shopping down there.

I remember when I worked in the Blackstaff we used to go into this wee shop every day and get sweets on tick. Then when you got your wages on Friday you went in and paid it.

And there was clubs in your works. And clubs in the mill, there was hairdressing clubs... shoe clubs... and tidley clubs.

My granny used to send me for snuff and you got it in a wee paper poke; you called the shop Soapy Joe's. A quarter of an ounce of scenty snuff.

You got scenty and you got plain. My Aunt Susan got plain and my granny was the same.

And chewing tobacco, my daddy used to get that ... a walking stick of chewing tobacco, and he smoked a pipe. You just cut some off and put it in your pipe.

Do you remember Sterlings? And then there was Goorwiches, and if you didn't get what you wanted in C&A you went to Goorwiches... or Sinclairs.

Aye, Sinclairs was a good one, it wasn't dear. I got my going-away outfit in there.

McMurray's was good; everything was on the floor.

You went there with your Provident cheque or your Standard cheque.

You know the simmets that the men used to wear? Where would you go to for a simmet† now? Or long-johns?

Aye, they done all that; she'd have brought them big boxes down.

I can tell you: McMurray's was missed when it closed.

My one wanted these 'high boy' trousers – high-waisted ones – and I took her into this shop on the Shankill, and I asked them if they had them. And I was told they had, but see when I produced a cheque, I was then told they hadn't. But I was still in the shop when this other woman came in asking for the exact same trousers, only she'd cash and I overheard him saying they *were* in stock. So I went over and near ate the arse of him!

Was his shop on the list? The cheque company gave you a list of shops that you could go to; the shop had to be on the list.

Yes, his shop was on the list. And I says: "Wait till I tell you, mate, see when my collector comes...!" I kicked up so much the manager had to intervene.

Getting those cheques still wasn't as bad as having to go to a money-lender.

You always got a bargain on the Shankill for coats and shoes, didn't you?

And Noble's for shoes.

I went to the London Mantle Warehouse on the Shankill.

I went to Quinns.

I worked with a girl from Orkney Street, she was an only child. She was Plymouth Brethren, and she got a coat for Easter and one for Harvest Thanksgiving – all the different church occasions. And she got them from a shop called Thompsons that sold lovely coats, just facing Canmore Street.

---

† Ulster-Scots word for a man's vest

That shop was 'up-market' for the Shankill, and their coats were all upstairs.

There's not really the same shops now.

In those days it would have took you a good half day to go down one side of the Shankill then up the other. But there's not really the same shops now.

No, it's just fruit shops mostly.

But there's shoe shops and all there. There's Kays Corner... and Stewarts.

Our wee corner shop in Clonard was owned by two sisters. And one of them, May Hoey, marked down everything you bought in a book. And she also had like a lodging house on the Springfield, and men working in Mackies stayed there. The standing area in the shop was tiny though, but it was a gossip corner too.

It was mostly people that came up from the country who run the corner shops. Locals hadn't got the money to start a corner shop. But these were all country people moved in because the work was here. And you remember the wee shop – Hamill's, was it? – where she made soda farls in her kitchen.

Aye, her husband had a big bike with a basket on it, and he went round the streets selling potato bread and soda bread and pancakes.

It was lovely too, wasn't it?

He sold apple cakes on a Sunday going up round Ballymurphy.

And that other wee shop in Dunmore Street; they'd a wee home bakery in theirs too – Turtles.

Their bread was beautiful.

We used to go down to Barney Hughes to buy broken biscuits.

And the fish man came round with his cart...

... with the cats running after him. As he gutted them he would have thrown them on the ground for these cats. And remember the herring man – 'Herrings alive!' – every Friday.

But your mother always baked, didn't she? Not necessarily big cakes or anything, just enough to do you.

Yes, nearly everybody's mummy baked.

And you knitted or did crochet.

And darned socks. My mummy got a bag out every night and done a weave and a heel; she bought wee bits of wool the same colour.

Sometimes the darns were awful hard though... they cut the feet off ye!

And then all the clothes were passed down the family.

Aye, you didn't know who originally owned the clothes you were wearing.

We once decided to perm our Mary's hair – remember 'Tweeney-Twink'? And she has red hair, so we permed it with that, and you put all them curlers in it. Well, you see when they took them out, God forgive me, we couldn't stop laughing, the curls just jumped out at us, she was like a photo of King Billy! And here's our Mary: "You've ruined my life!" She's thirty-six now, but she says she can still remember us all rolling about laughing at her. But you thought you were great, perming hairs and all. Ack, it was a geg.

That happened to my younger sister Lily. When she was still at school she wanted her hair permed, but my mummy wouldn't do it. However, she kept gurning and finally got a cousin to do it. But when our Lily came down the stairs it was like a thousand plaits let loose, and we all nearly died laughing. And our Lily said: "I'm not going to school!" but my ma said to her: "You wanted it, you got it," and made her go.

Housing and rationing

All the members of the group had been reared in houses which were quite different from those built today.

When we moved into our present house we thought it was great, we'd two toilets, one upstairs and one downstairs, and everybody was rushing to get to use the toilet at the same time – all seven of us!

We lived in rooms in Urney Street and my ma and da had five children, and they told my mother she'd too many children for a prefab and not enough for a house. But it was well known that by paying backhanders in them days you stood more chance of a house. In fact, there was a big scandal about it, and one woman who worked in the housing office ended up in jail.

Aye, that was known as the 'matchbox scandal', because if you put the money in a matchbox and pushed it across the desk you'd be looked after alright. This was in the fifties.

As a child I can remember one rent man commenting about the state of our rent book. And here's my ma: "Never you worry about the bloody outside of the rent book, it's the inside you worry about."

There was so little money about that very few newlyweds were able to move into their own home, the way they can do nowadays.

Aye, everybody lived up somebody's stairs round our way.

That's right, very few got moving into a new home straightaway. That didn't begin to happen until the 60s.

In my first house I hadn't even got a table; you just put a board over the child's pram.

Maybe the grandparents lived downstairs, and the daughter and her husband – or maybe the son and his wife – lived upstairs, you know.

Young ones don't do that now.

But then again, all the neighbours helped out, everybody helped everybody else.

There was more family support in them days; the grandparents especially did an awful lot of the looking after and rearing.

These days it's so different for young married ones: not only do they want a house all ready for them to move into, but they tell you what they want for their wedding presents – you get this list for Debenhams.

I know, it's unbelievable, isn't it?

We used to get basic wedding presents... like pillow cases, and we were glad of them.

I was given a mop and a bucket as one of my presents. And holy pictures.

The shortage of money was compounded, during the Second World War, by a shortage of food and other essentials.

I remember this woman who was pretty well off, she was a doctor's mother. And during the war, everything was rationed; you were allowed no more than about half a pound of sausages at a time. Yet she always seemed to have the best of meat – the butcher was only too happy to sell it to her. Anyway, this guy from the ministry came out to look at the butcher's books, and he seen that this woman had got this and that – she's was getting big steaks and all. And he come up to her house and asked her: "How did you get so much meat, seeing as it's rationed?" But seeing that he was a big fat man, she replied: "Well, by the look of you, you haven't been rationed either."

The only other way to supplement your rations was to go down to the 'Free State' and get things on the black market, then smuggle it home.

Aye, my mummy used to bring me with her, and manys a thing she'd have lopped around my waist under my clothes.

We all went there to get butter... usually from Drogheda.

Sure they used to organise bus runs down. 'Mystery Tours', that's what they called them.

Do you remember the sweetie coupons too? There was houses round our way and they used to sell the sweets and all, it was like the black market.

It was after the war that sweets really came in, Easter eggs and all that. We painted ordinary eggs for our Easter eggs.

Yes, my mummy dyed eggs for Easter too.

You were somebody if you had a chocolate Easter egg.

I always wondered what the fuss was about bananas, because you never got bananas. The boats couldn't get in during the war, and then when the first banana boat came in and some appeared for sale down the Springfield, people were queued up to buy them. And maybe you'd get three bananas. It was curiosity – people didn't know what they were like to eat.

And the Yanks were the ones who brought in the spam – I loved spam.

I liked the dried eggs, they were gorgeous.

And 'Aunt Jamima's Pancakes' – do you remember them?

Local characters
As one of the women said, "There are real characters in every area," and a few were brought to mind during the discussions.

Joe French died recently. He was a real character; he would have gone out every night to Gortnamona Club and had his nightcap of whisky and all, and at the final farewell there was a whole load of his family there – grandchildren and all – and they all got, even the wee ones, a wee 'nip' – egg-cups of whisky – and those who had doddies got their doddies dipped in it too! And they put the remainder of the bottle in beside him, and they all sang 'for he's a jolly good fellow'. That's what he wanted. And after the funeral there was a great do at Gortnamona Club, beautiful buffet, music... and that was the type of the man he was. It was a real Irish wake, so it was.

This was a wee woman on the Springfield, I was her home-help. She was brilliant to work for and her house was immaculate. She always loved everything new, whatever was the latest. And you know this thing now with your hair shaved up one side... she says she done that in 1920! And when she came home at night she put her hair in a middle shade and her mother never knew! She earned 2/6 a week – she was a lithographic printer – and she rubbed out the '6 pence' on her pay docket and gave her ma the two shillings – that left her sixpence to run about with. Out to St. Paul's Hall, all the dances, went with all the boys, she was a real laugh. She would say to her mother: "I'm going to my chum's house." And she would come in starving, and her mummy would say: "That was some chum, did she not make you a drop of tea?" Anybody who would come into the house, say the rent man or the meter man, she would say: "Hello son, any chance of your washing?" And the soldiers came in this day, running through, they were after somebody and she said to them: "What do youse want?" And one of them says: "I'm looking for a man!" So she says: "Sure, I've been looking for one for twenty years." She was a geg. She was really funny, and never no fighting or no argument out of her. Anyway, this morning I went and I couldn't get in. I rapped and rapped. And she was rarely out, except to get her messages or collect the pension. But eventually she opened the door and she had a towel wrapped around her head, and I said: "God, Mary, what's wrong with you?" She had fallen down the stairs and hit her head against a hall-table. And I said: "Show us it, Mary." And she took the towel off... and I near died! Her whole forehead just dropped down! So I rang 999, got an ambulance, and got her to the Royal. And we're sitting there, waiting to get attended to and this fella was sitting beside us, he was like a big docker. And here he was: "What happened to you, love?" Here she is: "The husband beat me up." And he said: "Where do you live!" He was ready to go round and beat this 'husband' up! Anyway, I'm waiting about an hour and finally here comes Mary linking arms with the consultant, and she had this big bandage wrapped around her head. Here's me: "Mary, we'll get a taxi." And she said: "Not at all, we'll walk it home." It must have been the drink kept her going. And with her dark glasses and this big head bandage – which she thought looked like a turban – she said: "Sure, don't I look like Jackie Onassis?" She was really great to work for, the best wee woman. When she took sick she said to me: "See when I die, Josie, I want to go up and into the Beehive when I'm dead." And I said: "Why, Mary?" She said: "Because I'll not be with them coming back, and I want them all to have a drink on me." Anyway, she died that March, but all her family were swanky – lived over in Bellevue and all – and they didn't like Mary not keeping up with them, and they certainly didn't want to set foot in no Beehive! Everybody loved her. She would say to me: "Would you go down to the doctors for me?" And I'd say: "What do you want, Mary?" "Spunking-up balls," she would reply. She was the funniest wee woman. She wore rouge and all and she had a wee wig. She said she was engaged three times but couldn't be annoyed getting married. I loved her.

There was another wee woman who was a great cook, I still have her recipe for scones. She was a silver-service waitress, wee Mrs Innis, lives in Highfield, well into her 80s now.

As a home-help you went from one house to the other. There was another wee woman and she was quite different; very nice, like, but very 'awfully, awfully'. And you had your table and your napkin; 'high tea' she called it. It was bloody well only lettuce and scallion and tomato, but she called it 'high tea'! She was awful nice, wore beautiful clothes. The wee woman facing her said to me: "I seen her changing three times a day, must have nothing else to do with her money." But she was lovely looking, and money was no option. She had a beautiful, real crochet dress, laced down to here, and she said: "When I die, I want you to dress me in that." I wasn't there when she died, but her daughter-in-law dressed her in it.

Bridging the divide... what divide?

The tragedy of today's communal divisions is made even more poignant when one becomes aware of how different it once was.

When John and I got married we moved to Dixon Street and my neighbours on both sides of me were Protestant. One used to crochet and knit baby clothes for my wee ones, and there was never any question of religion coming between us.

There were Catholics among the staff in Inglis's. And we'd all a great rapport.

Highfield was mixed at one time. Ballymurphy, New Barnsley, Dermott Hill – it was mixed then. But the Troubles brought fear, and that divided people.

Wee Jackie in our street was a Protestant. Worked in Mackies. He stayed the whole time; he was buried out of it. There was another girl who was a Protestant. But that never mattered to anybody. What mattered was that she had two lovely kids, and people were all over them. And she never moved from the area.

When you look back on all these families... Even our Angie's family, he was a Protestant.

My father was a Protestant, he came from Benview Street.

See every shop, from Merkland Street up on the Springfield Road, it was all Protestant owners. There was Billy Stewart, Lambs, there was the butchers, the wee hardware shop, the chemists, Turners, McAfee's, Bernie Spring...

Do you remember Midnight Dan – Dan Leckey – who worked in the laundry? He would have came all during the night for your laundry. He was awful fussy... gray hair, glasses.

That was Eileen Leckey's da, she worked with me in the Franklin Laundry. I worked in the Franklin Laundry when I was fourteen.

We had a cheque man, Paddy Murphy; we lived in the Shankill, and he come to our house for over twenty years, and I always went to Kashmir Road to make sure I got my cheque paid.

When we moved over here to Highfield we kept in touch with the ones in Ballymurphy 'cause there used to be a shop opened up there by Mina Kitchener, and my ma used to get her fags and tick there, she smoked Park Drive. And you used to have to go over there every two weeks. Then my mother started getting a wee bit scared going across and eventually lost contact. Although, when my mother died, there was someone came down from Ballymurphy to the house, they'd read it in the paper... but we had lost that contact.

It was fear, that's what it was.

Sure there's a family we knew and one of them was in the IRA and we're still friendly with them. They were at my brother's funeral a year ago, and they still keep in contact with us and we keep in contact with them.

It's sad the way the Troubles has divided people.

I think it depends on the way you were reared.

I never had any trouble with my family. Three boys and a girl, and I reared a nephew too, and never had any trouble with any of them.

I had six sons and it's a hard job. We live in an area where it is all paramilitary, yet none of them joined. It's just the way you rear them. It was a hard job keeping it all together but we did; none of them joined anything.

When we were young and starting work my father used to say to us: "Now, you're going out to work tomorrow – never take any part in any arguments over politics or religion. If anything starts, just walk away." That's what I've done all my life.

If you don't hear it in the house it's not in you.

Circumstances might change things – say if your father or bother got shot dead, that could change your opinion.

Some young ones are very easily led, they can get talked into a lot of things, no matter what they're taught in the house. And it's fear too. They're put under pressure to join these organisations... or gangs.

It's very hard. There's a family round our way who suffered terribly. One son was shot dead joy-riding, another was hit by a rubber bullet – he ended up with brain damage – and a third son was killed in a car crash. And their father was a good man; he had them kids in all the time, trying to keep them from trouble. But there was no law and order and it was impossible to watch them all the time. And that woman... oh, she just changed, completely, God love her. She's dead now, but she was a great wee woman.

Nobody rears their children and sends them out to do the things that have been done. They just get involved. And it's fear with a lot of young ones too.

I still ring Catholic friends to this day that I grew up with and worked together in the mills with, and we still ring each other. One of them lives in Andersonstown, on Shaw's Road.

I remember coming from school one day and I met the priest and he says 'good afternoon' to me, and I just looked at him... you know what you're like when you're young. And I went home and told my father about the priest and said that I didn't say anything back. And my father said: "You should have said 'good evening sir'."

There's very good people in every area but you don't hear much about the work they do. It's always ordinary people who hold areas together while the politicians collect their wages for prancing around and making a mess of things.

I worked in the C&A, and so did Margaret, and the rapport between Catholics and Protestants was fantastic – and still is.

We had one wee girl came to work with us and all you got out of her was 'Protestant this' and 'Protestant that', and I said to her: "Wait'll I tell you, love, we all get on well here together and we don't need any of your shit."

Both religions worked in the mills, and got on well together.

Everybody was in the same boat, as the saying goes.

When I was a home-help there were joint secretaries to represent the workers. I represented the Catholic side and Ellen the Protestant, and yet withal I went to the Shankill and represented the home helps there because Ellen lived down York Street. And we all went out on Christmas dinners together, we were all just ordinary working people. Inez McCormick once got us to apply for this award in Scotland, the Albert Armstrong Trophy – and we won it. That was in '84. They were just ordinary people, with no real education, but they knew how to get on together in a natural way.

Nothing revealed the genuine togetherness shared by the women than the empathy which was directed – by Protestant and Catholic alike – to one of their group whose family had suffered grievously when the IRA bombed Frizzell's fish shop on the Shankill Road. She had remained quiet during one of the discussions, the anniversary of the bombing weighing heavily on her mind.

I felt sorry for Lily last week. God help her. That was terrible – to lose four members of your family in two days – absolutely terrible. Her husband was being waked and her son and daughter-in-law went shopping for a wreath with their wee child ... and the fish shop went up. Just terrible.

How would you get over that? I felt awful sorry for her; I couldn't get it out of my mind. She was sitting there and I knew it wasn't her usual form. And she loved this other wee friend she always went about with, wee Beatsie, her husband was killed a while ago, and she loved her, the two of them were great friends. I said: "Youse two would make a good story." The two of them weren't bitter, neither the two of them.

See if anybody has one person in the family gets hurt in the Troubles, there's often four or five tragedies – in the one family.

You hear of that all the time.

The real divide in this society is between the haves and the have-nots.

And when you look at the television, there's fighting in nearly every country. We think we're bad but some of the other countries are far worse.

When you look at what's going on in the rest of the world you wonder why they're fighting here. We are lucky here – the poverty is terrible in some of those countries.

Stories of the 'Troubles'

Living through the Troubles evoked numerous reminiscences and anecdotes, some sad, some amusing.

> My son had to leave because of the Troubles. For a start, because of his age, he was getting stopped and hassled by the Army all the time. Then he became a taxi driver and his taxi was taken off him, along with another fella's. They had arrived first in the depot, and they were taken into a house, blindfolded, and their cars taken. The cars were being used for that break-out in Crumlin Road jail – although they weren't to know that. They were let out at 5 and told to go to Andersonstown police barracks. And they went up at 5 o'clock, but were told they had to come back at 7 when the detectives would be there. But when they went back at 7 they were taken to Castlereagh and held in there for four days! Then, whenever he got out he was getting stopped even more, so he came in one day and said: "Mummy, I'm going off to Dublin to live." And I said: "What about Mary and the youngsters?" He said: "I'll try and get a place as soon as I can." He was lucky; he was a plumber and he managed to get a house and Mary and the youngsters went down there. He did well; he has men working for him now.

> My son did the taxiing too. He got a call this time to go to the Dirty Diamond and he picked up this fare, went up onto the Shankill to go to the Glencairn estate. When they got to the bottom of the Glencairn the boys put a gun to his head and took the car off him. He only had it a few months, a lovely car, but they burnt it out. He had only £30 on him and they took that as well. But by the time he got it all sorted out with the Northern Ireland Office he was not the same man.

> Our Damien worked in Mackies, then when Mackies closed down he went to Galway. He's doing well now; he's an electrician.

> I sent my daughter one night down to the Rangers Club to phone for a Chinese. She was away that long I must have fell asleep. And when she came back I said: "Where did you get to? The Chinese never came." And she said: "Where did I get to! When I went down to the Rangers and rang the bell somebody shouts out: 'who is it?' And I shouts back: 'the bogeyman!' And this man opened the door and said: 'well, I am the bogeyman!' " He took her up the stairs with a gun to her head... they were robbing the Rangers, and

they had the staff lying on the floor! And when they left they locked everyone in and they couldn't get out. They were shouting out the windows for help.

There was this fella, he was awful nice – Trevor you called him, a Protestant fella – worked in our street. There was a builder's yard two doors from me, and he sat with all the fellas in the summer time when he was on his break, he was a lovely guy. And this Sunday morning there was a rap at the door and I went down and it was Trevor, and he had his tie in his hand and he was wrapping it all round and round. And I said: "God, Trevor, what's wrong with you!" And he said: "The IRA held me in Ballymurphy all night." They thought because he was working round there, but wasn't from the area, that he might be spying or something. But when they realised he wasn't they threw him into our street because he had told them he knew people there. I got Gerry up and he went over to a neighbour's who always had drink in the house, and the neighbour got him full – he needed the drink, he was still shaking! Gerry rung his wife and said: "Look, we've got Trevor, he's alright but we'll not bring him home yet a while." So they brought him home at four. He's a lovely man, and he walks up and down our road yet every day. He was a trade union guy.

One of my cousins married a guy from Limerick. Before they met this guy had joined the British Army – plenty of Free State fellas joined the British Army during the Second World War. But he was captured soon after he joined up, and ended up in a prisoner-of-war camp for five years. After the war he happened to be in Belfast before going to Limerick and he fell for my cousin – she was lovely, she was only eighteen. And they got married and they had a big family, but couldn't live in Limerick, they were starving... See that book – *Angela's Ashes*, by Frank McCourt – that is true.

People try to deny that that type of poverty existed.

In 1972, when the Troubles were really bad around the Springfield and Clonard areas, people were asked if they wanted to go away on 'a holiday' – it was another word for evacuating. We were told you'd be taken to Gormanstown where your kids would be well looked after. Everyone was talking about this and as I had eight kids I thought: 'great, we'll go.' The neighbours came round to help me pack. We all piled onto this bus and off we went; but instead of Gormanstown we ended up being accommodated at a mental hospital in Dublin – St. Brendan's. We didn't stay in the actual hospital building; we were put into a big house nearby, and we went over to the hospital to get our meals. We were given the basement of the house to stay in, so that we could all be together, and the people in the hospital would do our washing for us – although one day everything came back pink! There was a young girl there who was really pretty, with long dark hair, and she would come and take my youngest out for walks in Phoenix Park... the hospital was right beside it. After a couple of days one of the staff from the hospital told me that I shouldn't let this girl take the child out because she was actually a patient! So much for having the kids 'looked after'! I had a son born soon after we got home to Belfast and I called him 'Brendan' after the hospital.

At the start of the Troubles people thought that the church would be only too willing to support our communities, but the church was very slow to respond to people's needs, very slow, and they gave nobody any backing, for years. We had Bishop Philbin – 'fill the bin' they called him. He was from somewhere away elsewhere in Ireland, and he couldn't really understand our situation. You needed somebody who lived on the Falls to understand what was going on.

And Canon Murphy... that's why Des Wilson was put out of the church.

Yes, Father Wilson was a worker, and he never left the people of Ballymurphy. And they appreciated that.

And Canon Murphy put Mother Theresa out. She was getting too popular. There were jealousies there.

Father Reid was always level with people; so is Gerry Reynolds.

Our parents were innocent, they never had any hatred. You know the way when the soldiers came everybody was baking for them and all... and then there was an about-turn. One soldier went into the shop at Dermot Hill and asked for 20 cigarettes, and the girl said: "I'm not allowed to serve you." And he said: "But you served me yesterday!" She said she was afraid to serve him. And he said: "Well, you must be afraid of the IRA then." And she replied: "Well, so must you, when you're walking around with that big gun!"

My mammy used to put the empty milk bottles out on the front doorstep before going to bed, and this night wasn't a solider lying right across the entrance. And she said: "God, son, you frightened me there! You'll not have a kidney in your body lying on that cold ground..."

As if he was worried about his kidneys!

... "That's such a bad night to be lying on your kidneys, and your poor back and all... you'll not be worth a button." And he said: "Oh, I'll be alright, mam." And he probably wanted in for a wee warm, for he sprang to his feet and said: "While I'm here I'll go in and take your census"... you know the way they asked you who was in the house, and what ages they were, and all your business? And my mummy had a photo of the six of us on her cabinet, and he said: "That's a lovely photo, mam," and she said "that's my family." And he asked: "How many males have you?" but, with the English accent, my mummy thought he was talking about 'meals' – grub – and she said: "Well, when I get up in the morning about half-eight I get a wee drop of tea and a bit of toast. Then I make my way round to half-nine Mass and on the way back I drop in and get the *Irish News* and a bap for the oul' fella." And the soldier's standing looking at her in total bewilderment!

Then there was a fella went in to rob the post office down the Grosvenor, and he says: "Everybody up against the wall; you too, ma!"

And another time a gang went in to raid the bookies in Ardoyne and says: "Everyone up against the wall!" And one man says: "Jesus, no: that's the first bet I've got up." "Shut up and get up against the wall." So the gang grabbed all the money, but as one of them was going past yer man he asked: "What had you on?" And when he told them, the guy counted out his winnings, adding: "There you are; and we don't take tax!"

There was awful funny things happen. But that was what kept people living. Our street was a laugh, some of the things which happened. But it was very sad too, wasn't it? When you think back on all the people who lived there and how many of them have passed on. And even worse, all those who died in the Troubles, and all the young people who wasted their lives.

The shared experience of the blitz
The Second World War experience was one of communal solidarity.

We do a community lunch and we go into each other's communities – it's a good way to network. We seen some places in Clonard we never knew existed, like the vaults...

Yes, they have opened the vaults under the chapel for the month of November. That's where the people of Ashmore Street and Canmore Street all came in 1941. I was six years of age then.

That's right, every November they open the crypt, it's underneath the altar. And Protestants and all came to it, when the siren went they all came down from the Shankill.

I remember going to it with my mummy and you weren't allowed to turn on the lights because of the blackout. And you were going around in your bare feet...

I remember once the priest saying that anybody who lived in Springfield Avenue hadn't to go home – for Hitler had bombed Springfield Avenue. And Mackies, he was so near to getting Mackies... they done Cavendish Street and the brickyard, it got a bomb that night.

And Percy Street.

There was this family lived next door to us, there was fifteen of them, and God, they never got to the vaults, because their da said: "By the time I find fifteen the 'all-clear' will have went!"

And they said prayers all night until the 'all-clear' was sounded. What I didn't like was that your daddy brought you round, but they said: "Women and children only." So your daddy never got in, he had to go over to the 'Blackie' – you know, the Blackwater – and I was upset about that.

That's right, the men went down 'the Fields' – you know the Flush – and to the Blackwater – or else they went up the 'mountain loaney'... anywhere. Or the Falls Park. They just lay on the ground.

One man said that when he arrived at it he was told 'women and children only' and he looked around him, and there was no-one else there! It was a bit stupid when you think about it. There's the breadwinners threw out onto the bog!

Do you know what I can remember vividly? A wee woman running down the street and you know what she had on her head? A white enamel basin! That was her tin hat! I can remember that yet.

I used to cry, I hated it, and they sung these all-night hymns. You would be in it about two hours.

I was an evacuee with a couple out of Canmore Street and Ashmore Street, we were evacuated to Downpatrick, for six months.

Sometimes you just hid in the coal-hole – you know, underneath your stairs – and it was always lovely and warm there.

This night we could hear the family next door to us crying because their daddy was a firewatcher on Hugh and Dixon's Mill and the word had come through that it was on fire, and Mrs Meekin was squealing and crying in the coal-hole. And we could hear her, and here's my mammy: "I'll go in and see her." And as she went out, the airplanes were almost on the rooftops, they were circling round looking for Mackies. And they near got it... and they near got us as well!

Different generations

It was inevitable that the attitudes and behaviours of today's young people would be contrasted with their own experiences.

My daddy was strict, so he was, but being strict didn't do us any harm...

My daddy was in a wheelchair for fourteen years – he was 91 when he died – and we still had respect for him, we were afraid of him.

My da was left to look after seven of us. He worked in the shipyard then; he never got on a bus, he always rode a bike. And as he was cycling through the town if he saw anything in the shops cheaper than it was locally, even a ha'penny cheaper, you were sent down to get it. And at that time everything was rationed, like eggs and stuff, and if the shopkeeper gave us a small egg my da went over and demanded a big one. And he baked every Saturday, all different things, soda bread and stuff like that. And my sister used to bring us crab apples so he made jam, every morning he had that pot of jam sitting out for us, and he mixed the butter and the margarine up and we had it every day. And living like that didn't do us any harm, it certainly made me very careful where money was concerned. My father went to the pictures, the Stadium, every Saturday night, and he went to the graveyard on a Sunday... and that was it, he didn't smoke, didn't drink....

There was fifteen kids in the house next door to us – the Marleys – and their mother died when she was 35, and their father went out to work everyday. There was no such a thing as Family Allowance then, the nuns would maybe have come down and give them cooked ham. Yet they were all spotlessly clean; he had a rota written out for them, and they were all told what to do. I always admired him, he had to go out to work and then he came in and had to serve the dinner. Sometimes my mummy had to go in and separate the kids if they were fighting while he was at work, but they were always kept spotlessly clean.

Fifteen children? Imagine being 35 and having all those children. No wonder she died so young.

I suppose she was married when she was in her teens; she'd probably a child almost every year.

I used to clean my da's shoes for half a crown to go out to the dance, and you had to have them really polished.

I had to do my da's for nothing!

The men always loved their shoes really polished.

Our one said the other night that he wasn't going out because he'd only £40! By the time they pay their taxis and things apparently that's what it costs them each. I told him: "I reared youse all on £40 a week!"

My da went to the Stadium on a Saturday night and to the graveyard on a Sunday, and on Sunday night you had to get his suit and put it in all the folds and all and brush it and put it away. And whenever he was going out to the pictures you had to go and get the shaving mug, fill it up and bring it out, get his shirt, put his cuff-links in...

But men were spoilt then, and they were in control.

Now the women are in control, but it's going the other way. Some of the young ones today don't even have dinner ready for the men coming in from work. They wouldn't be bothered, they get a take-away or something they can stick in a microwave.

There's absolutely no sense of economy in young people these days. They laugh at me when I try to save money, but you can't help the way you were reared.

We're to blame for spoiling them! We give them what they want and if they ever hit bad times they'll not be able to handle it. Lean times wouldn't worry us the same way 'cause what we never had we never miss. Like, I've never been to Spain, it doesn't interest me, 'cause I was so content to be where I was. But young people today think they have to have their foreign holidays... but they're no happier, you know.

It's not so much the holidays, it's these designer labels on their clothes that they have to have – which I think is stupid.

One of my grandchildren is only five months yet he has to have 'Gap' everything. Here's me: "Sure he can't read, how does he know what he's wearing?" There's even designer labels on his wee shoes. Who the hell cares?

They all seem to think they're hard done by if they don't have those things.

I think today's parents will have to stop forking out money at some stage, 'cause these computer games are £100 each, and that's not on.

And the kids aren't satisfied with one.

In our day you filled your settee at Christmas time with nurses' uniforms, cowboy suits, toy sweetie shops, and they were all about five shillings each, isn't that right? You could fill your whole living room for £20.

I went to the market for all my family's clothes.

And I think they were happier times, so they were.

That's why you feel sorry for these kids today. They've all this stuff and they're not happy.

And the young ones today are bored. We were never bored, yet we didn't have anywhere near the range of toys kids have today.

You got an apple and an orange in your stocking at Christmas.

And you went to the swings or the park – Dunville Park – or you played street games: 'churchie one over', 'kick the tin', 'jack, show your light'...

That's right. And hopscotch.

I remember rapping people's doors at night and then running away.

The difference today is that they *kick* the doors now, and if you come out they're still standing there and they give you the fingers if you so much as look at them.

Children nowadays don't seem to know how to play those type of games.

The only games they seem to play are these computer games.

But that keeps them indoors; you don't see them out skipping, playing hopscotch or anything like that.

And if they do go out and stand at the street corners, then because they're not playing games, they look as if they're up to mischief.

That's true, that's the unfortunate part of it.

I blame the parents. You see wee babies in the pram wearing gold earrings....

Every time youngsters see something in the shop windows they're kicking and screaming that they want it.

I've heard of some even threatening suicide. They say: "If I don't get it I'll top myself."

Or: "I'll phone the child help-line, 'cause you're not allowed to smack me and you're not allowed to do this, that or the other..." You don't have to be cruel with children, but a wee smack doesn't do them any harm.

You have to let them know who's boss.

Even in school now the teachers can't discipline them now, they just talk back to teachers.

Some older citizens feel imprisoned in their homes because of the antics of certain young people in their area.

And there's all this bullying ... and all the different gangs too.

See the big estates... like, you hear terrible reports about Poleglass and Twinbrook: they build all those lovely houses but with no shops, no facilities, nothing for the kids to do.

They've got everything they want, the kids nowadays, they couldn't get any more, could they? They've the best of education and they've the best of clothes and they've the best of toys... and their CDs and videos.

Yet they're still not satisfied.

And they've all their own rooms. Yet with us, what was it? Three of us to a bed?

Well, there was three of us in the one bed.

But are they any happier? No.

One of the things they don't seem to like is work.

They don't want work, they want everything to be handed to them.

Our neighbour's young lad started work recently but packed it in after only four days. And they took £5 tax off so he says: "I want me tax back." And I'm thinking he'd be better to give himself a chance to get paying tax first!

And there's no neighbours now the way there used to be, most people close their doors now. They don't want you in, or else they're more concerned with whose house is the nicest. There's a bit of that spirit left, I suppose, but it's not the same as it was.

The younger generations haven't got the memories we would have; they will have no stories to tell, especially if they sit in the house staring at their computers.

And they don't sit and listen to the stories of the older generation. We've been running Christmas dinners for 20 years now and that's a time all our staff come in voluntarily, for they all get a good laugh and they're eager to hear all the reminiscences. But you don't get the younger ones sitting and talking with adults.

The sad thing is that I fear the present younger generation will not have all those funny reminiscences we all have – for they came out of our way of life, the sharing and the community spirit. That's disappeared to a large extent, and I think society has lost a lot because of it.

Island Pamphlets

1. **Life on the Interface** Belfast 'peaceline' community groups confront common issues.
2. **Sacrifice on the Somme** Ulster's 'cross-community' sacrifice in the First World War.
3. **Ulster's Scottish Connection** Exploring the many links between Ulster and Scotland.
4. **Idle Hours** Belfast working-class poetry.
5. **Expecting the Future** A community play focusing on the effects of violence.
6. **Ulster's Shared Heritage** Exploring the cultural inheritance of the Ulster people.
7. **The Cruthin Controversy** A response to academic misrepresentation.
8. **Ulster's European Heritage** A celebration of Ulster's links with mainland Europe.
9. **Ulster's Protestant Working Class** A community exploration.
10. **The Battle of Moira** An adaptation of Sir Samuel Ferguson's epic poem *Congal*.
11. **Beyond the Fife and Drum** Belfast's Protestant Shankill Road debates the future.
12. **Belfast Community Economic Conference** Grassroots groups explore issues.
13. **A New Beginning** The Shankill Think Tank outlines its vision for the future.
14. **Reinforcing Powerlessness** Curtailing the voice of ordinary people.
15. **Ourselves Alone?** Belfast's Nationalist working class speak out.
16. **Hidden Frontiers** Addressing deep-rooted violent conflict in N. Ireland and Moldova.
17. **The Death of the Peace Process?** A survey of community perceptions.
18. **At the Crossroads?** Further explorations by the Shankill Think Tank.
19. **Conflict Resolution** The missing element in the Northern Ireland peace process.
20. **Young People Speak Out** An exploration of the needs of Nationalist youth in Belfast.
21. **Puppets No More** An exploration of socio-economic issues by Protestant East Belfast.
22. **Beyond King Billy?** East Belfast Protestants explore cultural & identity-related issues.
23. **Are we not part of this city too?** Protestant working-class alienation in Derry.
24. **Orangeism and the Twelfth** Report of a cultural debate held in Protestant East Belfast.
25. **Broadening Horizons** The impact of international travel on attitudes and perceptions.
26. **Before the 'Troubles'** Senior citizens from Belfast's Shankill Road reminisce.
27. **Seeds of Hope** A joint exploration by Republican and Loyalist ex-prisoners.
28. **Towards a Community Charter** An exploration by the Falls Think Tank.
29. **Restoring Relationships** A community exploration of restorative justice.
30. **Separated by Partition** An encounter between Protestants from Donegal and Belfast.
31. **Left in Limbo** The experience of Republican prisoners' children.
32. **A question of 'community relations'** Protestants discuss community relations issues.
33. **Beyond Friendship** An exploration of the value of cross-border exchanges.
34. **Catalysts for change** A Los Angeles / Northern Ireland / Moldovan exchange.
35. **Dunmurry Reflections** Reminiscences from the 'outskirts'.
36. **Community relations: an elusive concept** An exploration by community activists.
37. **Living in a mixed community** The experience of Ballynafeigh, Ormeau Road.
38. **Cross-border reflections on 1916** Report of a cross-border conference.
39. **The forgotten victims** The victims' group H.U.R.T. reveal the legacy of 'The Troubles'.
40. **The unequal victims** Discussion by members of Loughgall Truth and Justice Campaign.
41. **Citizenship in a modern society** Report of a public debate.
42. **Whatever happened to the Peace Process?** Report of a public debate.
43. **Turf Lodge Reminiscences** Discussion by the members of Voices Women's Group.
44. **In search of a Haven** Discussion by members of HAVEN victims support group.
45. **An uncertain future** An exploration by Protestant community activists.
46. **An education for the future** Reflections on educational provision in North Belfast.
47. **Towards a shared community charter** Falls/Ballymacarrett Joint Think Tank.
48. **Reuniting the Shankill** Report of the Shankill Convention (May 2002).